T0015174

ROYAL COLLINS
RC
BOOKS BEYOND BOUNDARIES

SEE Noah's Ark Biodiversity Conservation Book Series

The Himalayan Honeybee

Written by Kuang Haiou, Zhu Xiaobo, and Yu Luyao   Illustrated by Liu Fudong and Li Sijia

SEE Noah's Ark Biodiversity Conservation Book Series

Cooperation Partner:

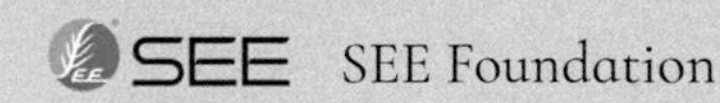

SEE Foundation

APSA

Nie Er and National Anthem Culture Education Base, XI-SHAN District, Kunming

Preface

The Southwest Project Center of the Alashan Society of Entrepreneurs & Ecology (SEE) initiated a program in 2013 for biodiversity conservation of the alpine forests in China's mountainous Southwest. Named SEE Noah's Ark, it is financed by the SEE Foundation in Beijing. Multiple conservation projects have been implemented by working with various stakeholders to protect endangered and rare species of flora and fauna, especially those with extremely small populations. It adopts solutions inspired by nature and advocates participation by the community, encouraging protection and the sustainable use of local biological resources.

The stories in the SEE book series: *The Asian Elephant*, *The Yunnan Snub-Nosed Monkey*, *The Green Peafowl*, *The Fish of the Jinsha River*, and *The Himalayan Honeybee*, all come from true experiences of front-line rangers and locals in conservation action. They are incredible. For both nature's characters and the people in the story, their connection to the native land and affection towards each other is rarely heard and miraculous in their own way. We then came up with a proposal to compile these lovely stories in a picture book to all our friends who have supported SEE conservation projects. They can be linked to real characters from dense woods and remote mountains, where heart touching stories occurred due to their generous support.

This picture book series is a group of works by conservation workers, scientists, sociologists, writers, and artists. The characters, environment, and neighboring creatures have all been carefully selected from real situations in our projects. In addition, explanatory notes of conservation are made to enrich the reading experience. We hope you enjoy it!

We extend our respects to those who have worked so hard to conserve their natural homeland, as well as to the SEE members and public who give donations to support these projects. These volumes are our gifts for the United Nations Biodiversity Conference COP15 held in Kunming.

XIAO JIN
Secretary of the SEE's Southwest Project Center
Chairperson of the SEE Noah's Ark Committee
June 2021

Data File: Himalayan Honeybee

Name in Chinese	喜马拉雅蜂 (XIMALAYAFENG)
Latin Name	*Apisceranahimalaya*
Alternate Names	Rock bee, Xueshan bee
Kingdom	Animalia
Phylum	Arthropoda
Subphylum	Mandibulata
Class	Insecta
Subclass	Pterygota
Order	Hymenoptera
Suborder	Apocrita
Family	Apidae
Genus	*Apis*
Species	*A. cerana*
Subspecies	*A. cerana Himalaya*
English Name	Himalayan Honeybee
Authorship	Maa
Distribution	Tibet, Yunnan

The Snowy Mountains are snow-capped all year around. Below the snowcap are lush green forests with all kinds of flowers blooming. The Hengduan Mountains in northwest Yunnan are full of vitality in spring.

"Buzzing, Buzzing, Buzzing ... Little bees, humming to work!"

Himalayan honeybees are vibrating among the flowers, sipping the sweetness to its full and enjoying the spring beauty. Here is Little Ya. He's a worker bee.

The Himalayan honeybee is a sub-species of Apis cerana, or the Chinese bee. It lives in the forests of high-altitude mountains on the southeastern brim of the Himalayas, where the mountains stretch to northwest Yunnan. Himalayan honeybees are mostly wild or semi-wild, thus they are cold-resistant, and are good at collecting nectar and pollen from a variety of flowers. They pollinate thousands of plants in the primeval forests of northwest Yunnan. It is one of the few bee species that can survive above 2,500 meters in altitude. They are the key to maintaining biodiversity and reproductive chains in alpine forests.

Belly filled with pollen picked, Little Ya followed the sun, which showed him the way back to the hive.

The nest was built in tree holes in the middle of the tree trunk. The natural tree hollow was tight and narrow, but was protective against wind and rain. It was comfortable enough to block the cold outside in winter. Everyone had been living like this all the time.

While approaching the nest, Little Ya found a group of wasps lined up, blocking its entrance. It looked like that the wasps were pouring out to engage in battle. Little Ya swiftly flew into the beehive through the "back door" and reported to the queen.

Northwest Yunnan has been home to numerous ethnic groups, including Tibetans, Lisu, Bai, Naxi, and Pumi, for many generations. Beekeeping has been a common practice for a long time. Traditional apiculture involves felling a large tree and hollowing it to form a bee barrel. And every time when harvesting honey, it will destroy honeycombs where the bees live. Not only is collecting honey troublesome, but the operation damages honeycombs, resulting in a low honey yield. What's more, the diseases and pests are hard to control.

When the queen bee, Mother Ya, heard the news, she said solemnly to all her children: "The wasps have attacked us too often and our colony has suffered heavy losses. The raid today here in such a combat situation. Let's retreat quickly. Otherwise, my dear children will be captured one after another and our colony destroyed!"

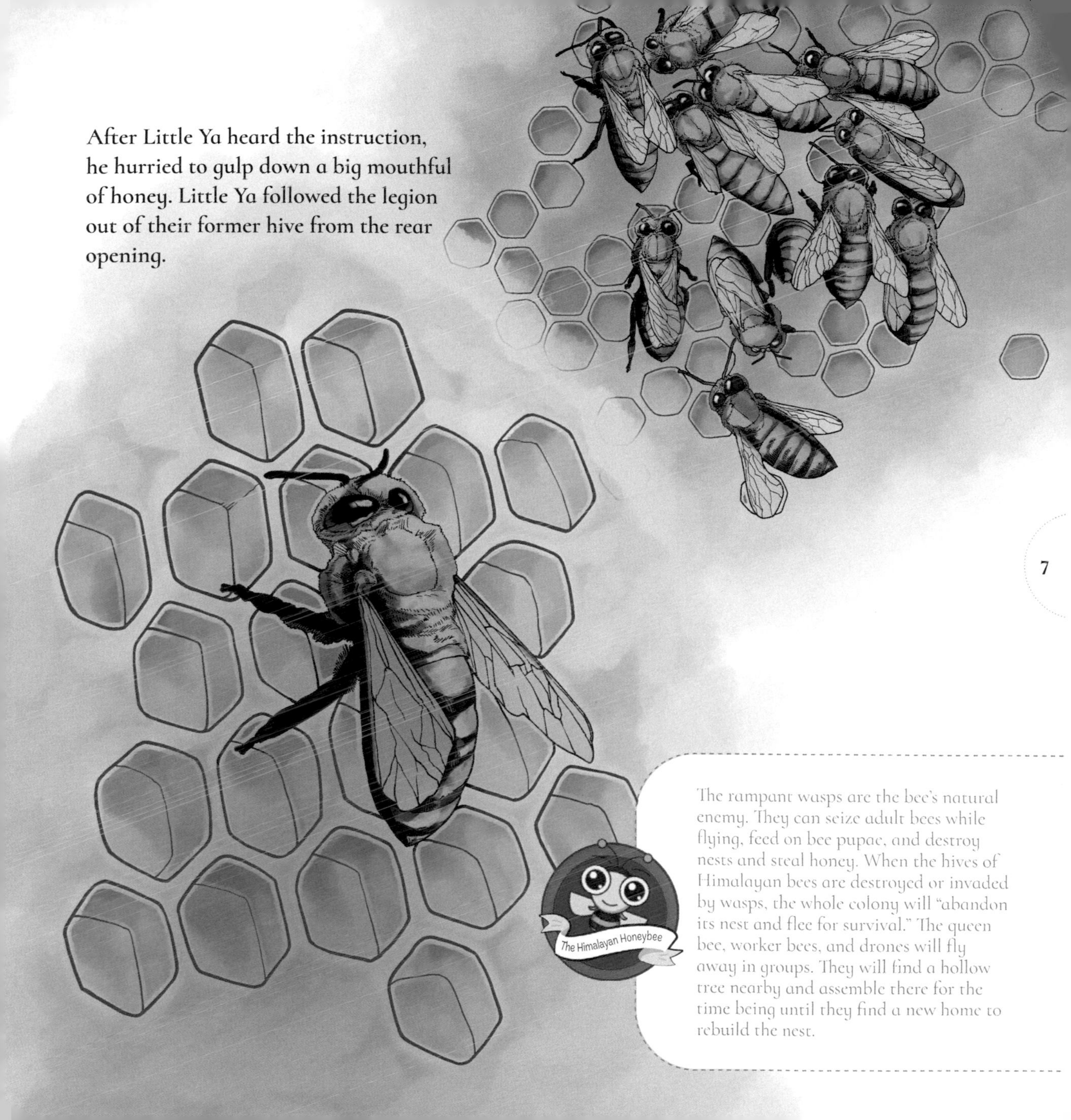

After Little Ya heard the instruction, he hurried to gulp down a big mouthful of honey. Little Ya followed the legion out of their former hive from the rear opening.

The rampant wasps are the bee's natural enemy. They can seize adult bees while flying, feed on bee pupae, and destroy nests and steal honey. When the hives of Himalayan bees are destroyed or invaded by wasps, the whole colony will "abandon its nest and flee for survival." The queen bee, worker bees, and drones will fly away in groups. They will find a hollow tree nearby and assemble there for the time being until they find a new home to rebuild the nest.

Little Ya and all the worker bees clung tightly to a big tree, surrounding the queen bee in the middle. This was a night they spent without a nest.

A scout team, out to look for a new hive early in the morning, returned rapidly with news: "Queen Mother Ya, there are some odd square boxes underneath a large tree not far from here. We saw many bee colonies nesting in the box, and there were few wasp nests nearby. Shall we try it?"

"Well, as other bees can live in a box, we may try it out as well! It is very good as far as there's no trace of wasps. Go again for a close look!" Mother Ya issued the order.

Honeybees are eusocial insects that live a highly organized life in the colony. They never move randomly whether out for nectar or migrating to a new home. The scouting bees are pioneers searching for nectar and pollens or new hive sites. When they find them, they will bring information back to the queen. With a decision, they will go to a new nest.

Little Ya and the colony flew into the empty wooden box. Little Ya weighed up his new home with delighted surprise. The box was clean and ordered, the size fitted perfectly, and the entrance for the bees was small and concealed so that it would not flood. There was a small shelter at the entrance for the worker bees to get into. The worker bees could take off and arrive with ease.

Queen Mother Ya directed Little Ya and all worker bees to take their positions immediately: gather the pollen and nectar, build up the hive. The width of the inner wooden frame is ideal for the honeycomb. Every Little Ya is a skillful craftworker. They cooperate with devotion and rebuild their beautiful honeycomb in hexagons.

The movable beehive is made up of a main chamber, upper cases, cover, beehive bottom chassis, honeycomb, a queen-protective net plate and other components. The parallel honeycombs are movable, making it easy to take them out for inspection and cleaning at any time. It is also convenient for beekeeping management, including harvesting honey, disease control and transportation.

Little worker bees were buzzing, buzzing, buzzing, hurrying up and humming to work!

Pretty soon, the hexagonal nests in the new hive were filled with sweet pollen and nectar.

On the hillside where Yunnan snub-nosed monkeys live, a variety of plants grow and bloom beautiful flowers. There are tall trees, such as *Cornus capitata*, *Viburnum betulifolium*, and wild cherry. There are shrubs such as rose, *Rhododendron*, *Coptis chinensis*, *Potentilla fruticosa*, and *Pyracantha fortuneana*, as well as medicinal plants like teasel root, *Radix phytolaccae*, *Herba moslae*, and *Elsholtzia rugulosa hemsl* . . .

Each kind of flower has a unique scent and color. The bees can detect every individual smell.

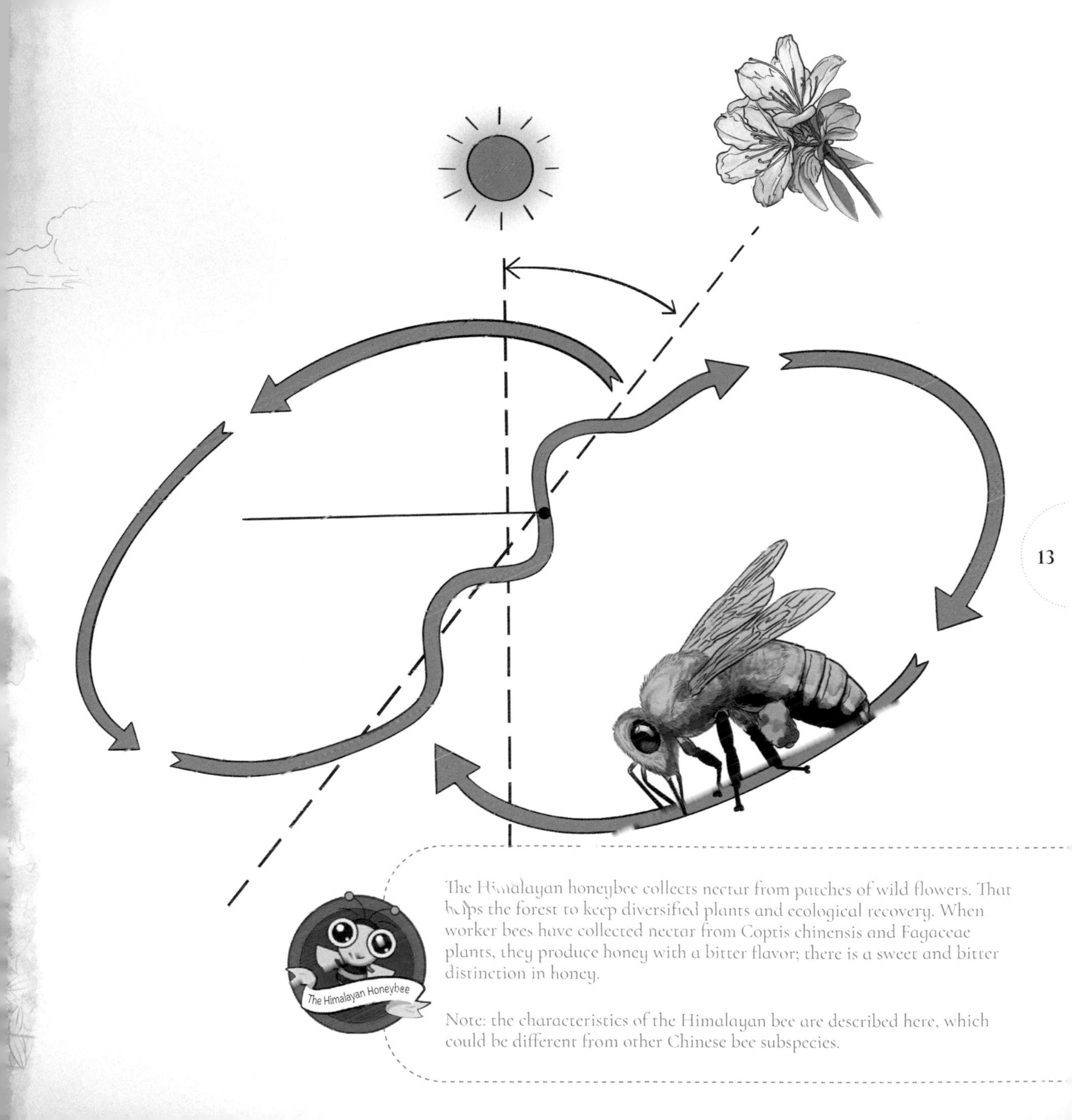

The Himalayan honeybee collects nectar from patches of wild flowers. That helps the forest to keep diversified plants and ecological recovery. When worker bees have collected nectar from Coptis chinensis and Fagaceae plants, they produce honey with a bitter flavor; there is a sweet and bitter distinction in honey.

Note: the characteristics of the Himalayan bee are described here, which could be different from other Chinese bee subspecies.

Now in the safe and comfy new home, Mother Ya concentrated on laying eggs. The workers kept growing stronger, and the family thrived. However, Mother Ya started to worry that she wouldn't have enough space for her new babies.

Soon enough, Mother Ya's worry was worked out. One day, Little Ya found a new case built above the main chamber with a net plate between so that Mother Queen, with a big, big body, could not go through. She just stayed in the massive chamber comfortably laying eggs. Little Ya and the worker bees could live upstairs and store nectar and pollen there.

The Himalayan honeybee generally has a lifespan of less than six weeks during the busy summer season and only a few months during the quieter winter season. However, the queen bee lives on average for two or three years and sometimes even longer. In order to maintain the size of bee colonies, the queen bee will lay eggs continuously. At most, she can lay over a thousand eggs a day.

In the early summer, a challenger turned up in Mother Ya's hive. A virgin queen had just hatched and wanted to make herself a new territory. If the virgin queen bee left, she would take away many young worker bees.

They didn't leave empty-handed but covered themselves with pollen and took honey with them. This way, they could build a home straight away once they found a new hive.

Mother Ya didn't feel sad. Those were her children. The more her children left to build their own colonies, the larger her family became.

The Himalayan Honeybee

The Himalayan bees are strong swarmers. A hive maintains a colony of about 15,000–35,000 worker bees. Searching for a new colony will occur as soon as the colony exceeds the upper limit.

A good life is always full of surprises and risks.

One day a mysterious thick smoke blew into the hive. Mother Ya and the workers felt dizzy. Everybody huddled into Mother Ya's main chamber. From the upper case, honeycombs full of honey were taken away by a pair of hands. Mother Ya watched as the hands put in another three honeycombs, one after the other.

She calmed down once the smoke was over. The eggs Queen Mother Ya laid in the nests were safe and sound, and there was plenty of nectar and pollen for the young bees to hatch in the main chamber.

"Anyway, thousands of my Little Yas will soon be able to construct a new honeycomb in the upper case and fill it with nectar and pollen!"

Locals have an ancient history of apiculture. Honey is an excellent source of nutrition in the alpine and semi-alpine regions. A local saying goes, "It is better to have no rice in the pot than no honey at home." There are more than 60,000 colonies kept in Weixi Lisu Autonomous County, which is a nature reserve for Himalayan honeybees. The county also holds a honey market for distribution in northwest Yunnan.

The winter came early this year in northwest Yunnan. The temperature dropped quickly. The beekeeper cleared out bugs creeping into the hive and "placed" a layer of thatch around it to provide insulation. The bees had with them an additional upper case fully-stocked with honey.

Crowding around their Queen Mother Ya, worker bees tried to rest over the winter, enjoying the sweet honey due to their labor. In a stormy winter, 3,600 meters in elevation at Baima Snowy Mountain, Mother Ya and her children all needed a safe and warm home such as this.

They look forward to a beautiful spring in the year ahead.

Bees huddle together for warmth. Those who have sipped honey would go to the outermost layer and flap their wings to produce thermal energy to keep the crowd warm. Bees in the centre will take turns to squeeze to the outside, replacing their companions. This well-organized order allows the bee colony to maintain warmth and circulation inside the hive.

About the Authors

Kuang Haiou is the director of the Institute of Apicultural Research at the Yunnan Agricultural University. His major research interests are bee behavior study, bee machine science, bee breeding and management, bee culturology study, etc.

Zhu Xiaobo majored in apiculture studies at the Fujian Agriculture and Forestry University. His work includes the technical training of beekeeping and endangered medicinal plant breeding.

Yu Luyao is a staff member at the SEE Conservation Project Center. He studied biotechnology and joined SEE in 2016, working in biodiversity conservation in Southwest China.

Liu Fudong, born in the 1990s, is an experienced illustrator who graduated from the product design department of Yunnan Arts University.

Li Sijia, born in the 1990s, is an experienced illustrator who graduated from the visual communication department of Yunnan Arts University. She has worked as an illustrator in the Kunming Zuodao Enterprise Marketing Strategy Co., Ltd.

SEE Noah's Ark Biodiversity Conservation Book Series

SEE: The Himalayan Honeybee

Written by Kuang Haiou, Zhu Xiaobo, and Yu Luyao
Illustrated by Liu Fudong and Li Sijia

First published in 2023 by Royal Collins Publishing Group Inc.
Groupe Publication Royal Collins Inc.
BKM Royalcollins Publishers Private Limited

Headquarters: 550-555 boul. René-Lévesque O Montréal (Québec) H2Z1B1 Canada
India office: 805 Hemkunt House, 8th Floor, Rajendra Place, New Delhi 110 008

ISBN: 978-1-4878-1081-8

To find out more about our publications, please visit www.royalcollins.com.